Fail

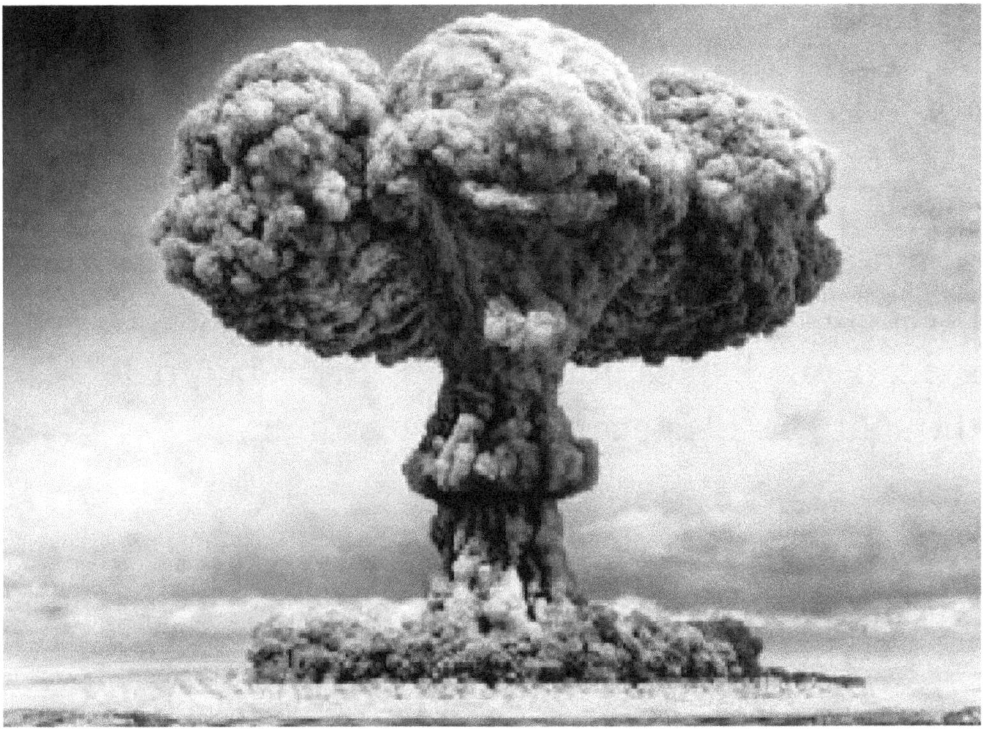

Failure, just means you have to try it a different way!

In the late 1990s, I was the first people I know of who created an audio CD outside of the record industry. I had an idea that in the future, all video would be digital and distributed either through the internet or on CD's / DVD's. I then formed a company called DRD, Digital Rights Distributors, which would make the videos into DVD's or CD's.

I approached the professional speaking industry with the concept of taking their 35,000+ speaker membership, each with dozens of videos on VHS video tapes, and convert them to digital CD's and DVD's. Once converted to digital, I could distribute them from a central web site for potential customers to review their content and presentation style. This concept was a success in the auto-malls, restaurant rows, and retail malls. I thought this idea seemed like a winner.

The speakers never felt comfortable with this concept and convincing them was impossible. Eventually I came to the conclusion that while the idea was sound, the speakers perceived each other as fierce competitors. They would never concede and allow their videos on a sight with another speaker's videos. Unfortunately, fear that a potential client would visit to this site to view their video, giving the client the opportunity to to choose the competitor.

Today, speaker bureaus list hundreds of speakers and their videos on each of their sites without any concerns whatsoever. It was about a decade too early.

Success

"Success is continuously trying until you succeed."

The biggest success was a company I built around creating the very first voice recognition, which eventually led to Dragon Dictate and Siri. I also pioneered voice synthesizing (also the forerunner of Siri), home automation, and the HeadMouse and other computer input devices. All these inventions lead to creating "The First Computer To Save A Human Life", as coined by Steve Jobs.

That original prototype along with 18 other inventions are now part of the permanent collection of the Smithsonian Institution in Washington, D.C. including 30,000 of my personal papers. There are another 14 inventions located in the Computer History Museum in Mountainview, CA. I am also the bestselling author of "The Social Media Bible", which hit #1 on Amazon, is in five languages and its Third Edition along with my latest bestselling book "The Fusion Marketing Bible", which hit #3 on Amazon and in now in three languages.

Throughout this learning curve of career trial and error, I learned invaluable lesson and gained insights. The most valued lessons learned came from my failures more than from the successes. The successes took care of themselves. They took place either because of me or in spite of me. The failures taught me the hardest and most valuable lessons, which resonated throughout the rest of my career. See www.LonSafko.com.

Here are The Top 10 Lessons To Entrepreneur's Success, with many of my original "quotes" developed to be your guide to those lessons

10. Observation

"Solutions are observing the same information, uniquely."

Pay attention to things going on around you. Watch the industry. Watch for changes. Look for trends. Study the competition. Learn their successes and failures so you don't repeat them. Watch the news and analyze each story for how it can affect you and your company. I lost my largest round of venture capital from the UAE disappear the morning George Bush Senior invaded Iraq on

August 2, 1990. I watched my investment vaporized on the national news.

Have you ever observed "the moon sometimes comes out in the day, but the sun never comes out at night", or "Why is the word 'short' longer than the word 'long', or "Why does mathematics give preferential treatment to even numbers? Odd x odd is odd, even x even is even, and even x odd is even.", or "If it wasn't for your belly button, every morning you would wake up covered with lint." Be aware of what's going on around you.

Insight: Pay more attention to other industries than your own. Henry Ford is credited with changing manufacturing forever by inventing the conveyor belt. Henry didn't learn about the belt from Gottlieb Daimler, Louis Chevrolet, Karl Benz, or Ransom Olds, at the time. He was eating his lunch one day on a potato farm, watching the potatoes going up the belt from the ground to the truck. If the solution you needed existed in your industry, you would have already be aware it. Observe.

9. Change

"Change forces growth."

I am a strong proponent of "If it ain't broke, brake it!" Not my quote, but true nonetheless. Einstein once said "The definition of insanity is doing the same thing the same way and expecting different results." So often we are stuck in that mode or rut. Often, I would deliberately change things up to see if I like the different results better. If not, I could always go back to doing it the same way. In nearly every case, the results did prove to be better. "Sometimes you have to just color OUTSIDE of the lines."

The more you voluntarily embrace change the easier it is for you to adapt to change when it's unanticipated. The only thing that remains constant is change itself.

Insight: In 1872 when George Eastman founded what was to become the Kodak Company in 1892, he believed that the film camera would last forever and, it nearly did, about 125 years. It had a good run. No one at Kodak believed that digital photography would eliminate the need for processed film; however, in the late 1990s the revolution began. Too slow to adapt to this technology, Kodak resisted this change until they were all but forced out of business by the digital camera. Now, the digital still and videos cameras are being forced out of existence by the smart phone. "Change is inevitable, anticipate and embrace it."

8. Attitude

$$1 + 20 + 20 + 9 + 20 + 21 + 4 + 5 = 100\%$$
$$A\ T\ T\ I\ T\ U\ D\ E$$

"Your attitude sets your course."

A positive attitude isn't a plus, it's mandatory. Success is more than just a positive attitude; it's about having an attitude of believe. You must always believe in what you do, believe that you will succeed. Your attitude becomes your beacon. Your light that you send out to others that will guide them into shore and make them feel safe in you and your vision.

"You have to be positive to have a positive attitude." You can't let defeat, setbacks, conflicts, finances, mistakes, or unforeseen obstacles get you down. "It's not about making mistakes as much as it is how you correct them.", and "Don't worry, a year from now you won't even remember the details of the problem that has you worried.", and "If not for mistakes, humans would not have evolved."

Insight: I was sitting in a Starbuck's and at the table beside me was a manager training 3 new hires. I overheard her saying when a customer comes up and orders a coffee and doesn't use our size names Venti, Grande, Tall, & Short; because they cannot remember them or they that may think they are pretentious, it's not our job to correct, embarrass, or to teach them. It's our job to get them the coffee they want.

Wow! I'm one of those people who refuse to use their nomenclature when ordering. I do consider their names pretentious. They were referring to people like me. Remembering back, no one has ever "corrected" me. They just smiled and got me the coffee that I wanted. It's all about attitude. That's why I patronized Starbuck's where I overheard that conversation. Attitude is everything.

7. Weaknesses

"Admitting your weaknesses is your strongest strength."

Know your strengths, but more important, know your weaknesses and surround yourself with people who's strengths reflect your weaknesses. You are good at what you do. Don't kid yourself into thinking that you are good at everything. If I wanted to be an accountant or a doctor, I would have changed my course studies in college. You are who you are for a reason. You might be great at many things, but one person can't be great at everything. The sooner you realize this, the faster you are on your road to success.

Insight: I had the pleasure of working with both Steve Wozniac and Steve Jobs. Jobs at Apple and The Woz at the company he formed after leaving Apple, Cloud 9. The two Steves were so successful with their original idea, the P.C., Personal Computer (first coined by Steve Jobs), because they were SO completely different in every way. Jobs was demanding, domineering, ruthless, and knew what people wanted before they knew themselves and Woz knew how to build it.

The two personalities were diametrically opposed, but complimented or "completed" one another. And, they knew that about themselves right up until the end. It was that strengths & weaknesses formula that propelled Apple to the world stage. Recognize your weaknesses and surround yourself with people that exhibit those strengths. "You won't be good at what you do if you don't like doing it." Surround yourself with strength.

6. Vision

"You have to be in the game in order to win!"

People follow leaders with a positive attitude and a clear vision of success. Develop a clear vision of what it's like to win, then you will be able to share your vision with the same passion you feel with those around you.

Whether it's A.J. Foyt* and the finish line at the Indianapolis 500, Mean Joe Greene** and the Super Bowl goal post, or Edmund Hillary** and the top of Mt. Everest, your team needs a leader who will show them the way to victory. Behind each of these great achievers were great teams that shared their vision.

Some days you will wake up and say screw that vision, and that's OK. Just walk it off and show up with enough enthusiasm for everyone, whether you like it or not. It's not a choice. When your team trusts you to take them over the finish line, they will follow whatever vision you have. If it's to the pits or if it's to the Winner's Circle, they will take you there.

* A.J. Foyt with 4 Indianapolis driver-owner victories.

** Mean Joe Greene with 6 Super Bowl rings; 4 as a player and 2 as a personal assistant.

*** Edmund Hillary was the first to scale Mt. Everest at 11:30 a.m. on May 29, 1953.

Insight: When I created The First Computer To Save A Human Life, I knew what it should look like years before I created it. Having the vision of the finished product in mind, all I had to do was build towards that vision. Having a clear vision of the end result is paramount. If you can see your success, others around you will too. Stay laser focused.

5. Communication

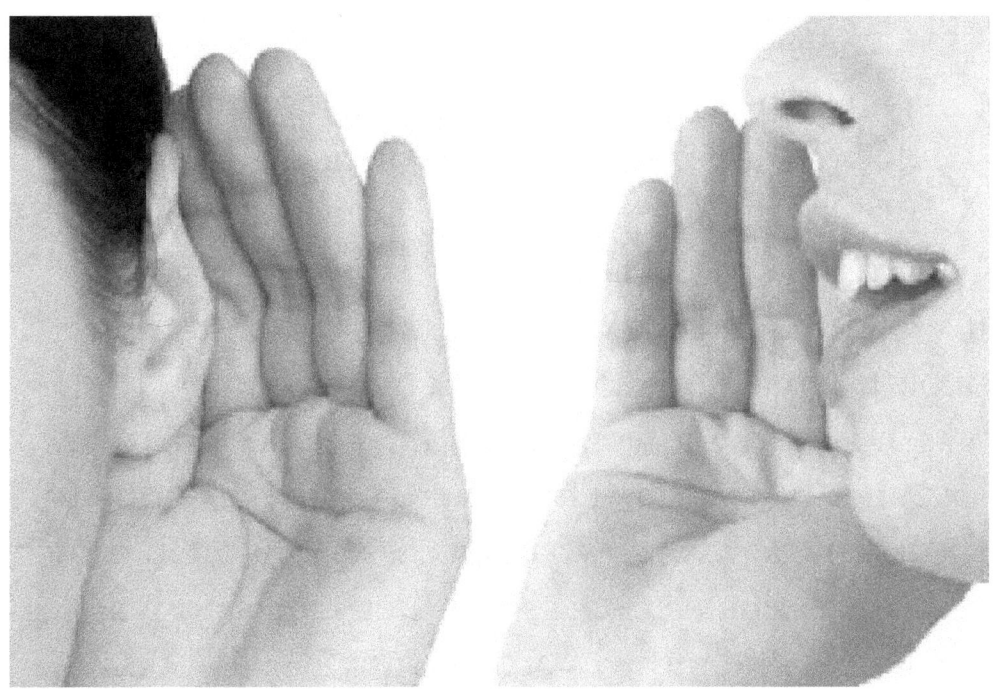

"When you want to know what someone is thinking, all you have to do is listen."

Open and frequent communication is critical. You must always be sincere, authentic, and transparent, because if you aren't transparent, your team will see right through you.

If you want your team to share your vision, then it's your responsibility to communicate that vision to them, clearly and often. If that vision of success is blurred then your team's vision also gets blurred.

"If you want to hear the answers, sometimes all you have to do is listen to the silence."

Insight: Nearly every morning, no matter how busy it was to be the entrepreneur, I would visit each department in the company; engineering, warehouse, manufacturing, software design, sales, and administration. There were three questions for the team to answer; what successes did the have yesterday, what set backs did they face, and what can I do to help the overcome any roadblocks. They always knew that it was my responsibility to remove their roadblocks.

This took time and much of the next lesson; trust. But, once they trusted me, they communicated openly, which lead to greater productivity and creativity, making their jobs much more rewarding and of course, this led to an increase in revenue. Communicate clearly and often.

4. Trust

"If I don't trust you to do your job, I don't need you."

Trust yourself, and others around you. If you follow the weakness lesson from above, you will surround yourself with the best, complimenting skilled people you can find. Trust them. If you don't trust someone in your organization to do their job... Get rid of them and find someone you completely trust. "It's impossible to do your own job well if you are constantly doing someone else's."

Counsel with those you trust. Solicit their advice; however, ultimately, you are the one that is responsible for your company, and team. You alone will be judged for your decisions. Always take the high road and trust your own integrity. "You can never go wrong doing the right thing!"

Insight: "You will always make the best possible decision with the information available" or "If you can't make an important decision, decide not to decide. You don't have enough information." Trust yourself that you will make the best decision possible. You're smart. Wait until you have new information, so you can make a more informed decision. And, never regret a past decision no matter what the outcome. It was the best decision you could have made with the information you had at the time. Trust yourself.

3. Passion

"Four qualifications for success; training, experience, talent, and passion."

Follow your passion. The money will follow you. As I mentioned above, if you aren't passionate about what you are doing, you will never be excel at it. "Find you passion and follow it with a passion."

Insight: When it came to developing solutions for the physically challenged, I was passionate. I would wake up in the middle the night and grab my bedside pad, jot ideas down in the dark, and build them the next day. Doing this over and over until more than 125 individual products for the disabled were developed. Being passionate about finding solutions drove me to excel.

Many of these designs you see today are taken for granted. Just one example is the little balloons that pop-up when you hold your cursor over a button for a second or more. It was created on March 6, 1986 and first called "Balloon Help", then eventually "Tool Tips". The creation was important, because the severely disable were unable to hold a spiral bound paper user's manual. Be passionate about what you do.

2. Innovation

"Innovation: Mixing common elements to form an uncommon solution."

This is a tough lesson of for a majority of people to learn. Learning to be more innovated can be high on your list, but difficult to understand. For some, it just comes easy and happens all the time. Others find, it's a learned skill like riding a bike or playing the piano. Some are just better at it than others; however, everyone can be better at it than they are.

Several years ago, I wrote an article about the actual process of innovative thinking and how it works. You can find that article here: "The Three Cs Of Innovative Thinking", published by Lon Safko on Amazon in both eBook and paperback formats.

Insight: I am constantly being innovative. Innovation isn't just about the copyrights, inventions in the Smithsonian, or U.S. Patents. Innovation is a daily occurrence. Here are a couple of examples:

- Want to keep your kitchen trashcan liner from falling in the can? Loop 6 rubber bands together and connect them with a paperclip to form an elastic loop.

- Want to keep your garden hose from tangling? Don't coil it over the holder, loop it back and forth.

- Want long extension cords from tangling? Tie it up in continuous slip knots (Sinnet - look it up!), the way mountain climbers do.

Innovation is all around us. There are numerous ways to view innovation: "Innovation happens by combining common elements to form an uncommon solution", and "Innovation is perceiving information uniquely", and "An intellectual can discern patterns; a genius can discern patterns where none are obvious; an innovator can discern patterns where none exist.", and "Inspiration is when two or more common concepts fit together to form a unique solution."

And, the number one Top 10 Lessons To entrepreneur success I learned in my journey as a entrepreneur:

1. Tenacity

"You can't loose, if you don't to quit!"

This is my most important lesson learned as a entrepreneur... Never... Give... Up!

Whether it's engineering or sales, art or marketing, "No doesn't mean no until there is a restraining order.", and "Failure, just means you have to try it a different way!", and "Success equals a little vision, followed by a great deal of tenacity!" How many different ways can I say it?

Insight: All of the successes in every company I've ever built, required undaunted tenacity, every day, in the face of every failure. My #1 lesson learned is the most true. You can't loose if your don't quit. (Worth repeating.)

Believe in what you are doing, be passionate, trust those around you, communicate your vision, trust yourself, embrace change, pay attention, maintain your positive attitude, but the most important lesson you must adhere to is... Never give up!

For more information about the author, please visit www.LonSafko.com

www.ingramcontent.com/pod-product-compliance
Lightning Source LLC
Chambersburg PA
CBHW050038230526
45470CB00003B/1338